Classic Pickups

INTRODUCTION

Left: *George Yackey worked for Case and bought this Ford F-1 truck new in 1949. From then until 1971 it was used as a farm machinery service truck. The Colorado summer sunshine has faded the paint from its original red to burnt orange.*

THE PICKUP TRUCK is inextricably linked to the development of America itself. As surely as the horse and the shovel, so the pickup truck has helped shape a land and a nation. The history of the truck starts with the transition from horse to the internal combustion engine as the prime source of motive power. Where the history will end is unknown but it's no accident that there is a 1936 Ford truck in the *Star Trek Voyager* TV series. The program-makers, looking for something that encapsulated twentieth century America featured a pickup truck drifting through space. This gives an indication of how far the pickup has worked its way into the American consciousness.

As well as having shaped America, the history of the pickup can be seen as a microcosm of the history of the twentieth century. There were pickups working on farms on the day in the spring of 1917 that the *Lusitania* was torpedoed off Ireland, and America entered the war. There were Chevy pickups hauling bootleg liquor through the Prohibition era, Ford pickups hauling rapidly devaluing goods after the 1929 crash on the New York Stock Exchange and a beat up truck hauled Tom Jaud and his family west to California. There were pickups engaged in the construction of the Hoover and Grand Coulee dams as America worked its way out of the Great Depression. Pickups were carrying service personnel about their business on the day that the skies above Pearl Harbor filled with Mitsubishi Zeroes, and Dodges and Jeeps splashed ashore on Pacific Islands. Dodges and GMCs hauled the GIs of the Allied Army across Europe. Trucks had a place in the changed postwar world too; the guy who delivered parts from the local Case dealer brought tractor parts out to the farm in one of them new Fords. Trucks evolved in response to the gas crisis of the early seventies, and in the eighties and nineties trucks were decreed to be cool and a lifestyle evolved around them. Slammed minis and outrageously tall 4x4s vied for attention at shows while mainstream pickups became ever more luxurious and competed with sport utilities and station wagons in dealers' showrooms across America.

Each chapter of this book opens with a quote that sets the pickup truck in the context of that particular decade. It's no surprise that pickups are mentioned so often, just as it is unsurprising that vintage and classic trucks are still being driven, restored, and street rodded as well as being regarded with such affection. There's no doubt about it, a pickup is a whole lot more than "just another means of transportation."

Above *Through a succession of careful owners, this 1925 Model TT one-ton closed cab truck has survived almost as it was when new. Note the wooden spoked wheels and grain-carrying load bed.*

No sooner had the three trucks left town than Rusk appeared in his pickup, accompanied by Dewey Kimbro, and when the new newpaper editor shouted: What's Up? Rusk cried back: We're spudding in an oil well.

TEXAS. JAMES MICHENER (1985).

BEGINNINGS

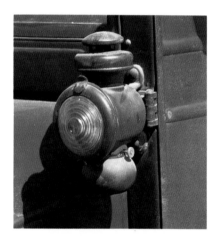

IN TEXAS ON JANUARY 10, 1901 something happened that helped the internal combustion engine progress ahead of horses, steam and electricity as the primary source of power for vehicles. The huge Spindletop oilfield produced crude oil for the first time on that date and from the liquid black gold came kerosene, paraffin, naphtha and later, crucially, gasoline. The early history of the pickup truck is inextricably intertwined with that of the first automobiles. In exactly the same way as there had been horse-drawn vehicles for carrying people and horse-drawn vehicles for carrying goods, from the earliest days of the motor industry there would be machines designed with both these separate purposes in mind.

As early as 1900 there were four large automobile shows held in the US. In this year shows were held in Bedford, Connecticut, Chicago, Illinois, Trenton, New Jersey and at New York's Madison Square Garden. The latter event was by far the largest featuring 300 vehicles from around 40 manufacturers and was run under the auspices of the Auto Club of America. The now more well known Automobile Association of America was founded in 1902.

Oldsmobile is acknowledged to have built the first factory specifically intended for motor vehicle pro-

duction in 1901. Simply it was forced to rebuild its factory following a disastrous fire which all but destroyed the business. In the wake of the fire, in order to resume production it started sub-contracting for many of the components used in its production of cars, something that is now widespread in the auto industry worldwide. In the 1900s the US population numbered approximately 76 million people of whom the majority lived in rural locations. Roads existed but only 150,000 miles of them could be described as "improved" at the time. Improved did not mean surfaced as only 150 miles of the improved total were actually hard surfaced.

Many of the companies who would flourish in the early years of auto manufacture were already established making related items such as agricultural machines.

The International Harvester Corporation (IHC) had its beginnings in the McCormick reaper of 1831 which subsequently led to the formation of IHC in 1902. By 1907 the company began production of commercial vehicles and vehicles such as the Auto-Wagon which offered a choice of panel truck and grain box bodies were being produced. Through the remainder of the decade the company went on to produce a range of light trucks including utility wagons and panel trucks but gradually shifted its emphasis wholly to light trucks. A new line of conventional trucks was introduced in 1915 with payloads ranging upward from three quarters of a ton.

Studebaker's involvement with light trucks also pre-dates the advent of the motor vehicle – the company had been manufacturing horse-drawn commercial vehicles in South Bend, Indiana since 1852. Henry and Clem Studebaker had a blacksmith's shop in South Bend where they made wagons for local farmers. From this humble beginning evolved a noted horse-drawn vehicle manufacturing operation and by 1876 the company was a large concern. After experimenting with some early automobile designs and electric propulsion around the turn of the century it finally introduced an internal combustion engine powered automobile in 1902. Studebaker subsequently cooperated with other fledgling manufactur-

ers including the EMF Co and Flanders but by 1914 the company was sufficiently established to introduce a light commercial vehicle of its own, the three-quarter-ton Model Three Delivery Car. This truck was available in two forms, panel or an express delivery, basically a van or a pickup. These machines were powered by an in-line four cylinder engine of 192.4 cubic inch displacement, achieved through a bore and stroke of 3.5 x 5 inches and produced 30 hp. The vehicles remained in production until in 1918 Studebaker discontinued all commercial vehicle production.

The now massive GMC corporation had started in an equally small way; in 1903 William C. Durant took control of Buick and in 1908 founded the General Motors Company which absorbed a number of other early car and truck makers. Starting in 1911, the same year as GM shares were listed on the New York Stock Exchange for the first time, the company's trucks were sold as GMC models. By this time devel-

Right: The closed cab was an option first offered on the Model TT in 1925. Other options included the windshield wiper, battery headlights and 30x5 inch rear tires, all of which this truck has.

Left: The Model TT was powered by a 176.7 cu in displacement L-head engine. A choice of Kingston or Holley carburetors were fitted. This engine has had a crack in the cylinder head welded and is original apart from the new Champion sparkplugs – Champion still make plugs for Model Ts.

vehicles diverged. This was seen as a mixed blessing due to the lessening of spares interchangeability. Chevrolet pulled ahead in terms of sales in 1927 with the best selling truck in America and so the long-running Ford versus Chevrolet rivalry began.

Ford discontinued the long production run of the Model T, affectionately referred to as the "Tin Lizzie," having produced in excess of fifteen million vehicles. The Model T was replaced by the Model A in 1928 and Ford soon regained the sales advantage when the Model A car and the Model AA truck started coming off the production lines. The Ford Model AA, half-ton models were available as both Roadster and closed cab pickups and by 1931 there were 31 different colors of Ford truck available. Although this gave Ford the lead, the Wall Street Crash hit in October 1929 and devastated America's economy. The Crash would lead to the Great Depression which would last into the thirties and see an estimated 13 million Americans out of work by 1932.

By 1928 Chevrolet had become a major threat to Ford's dominance of both the car and truck markets. In the last year of the decade Chevrolet produced its half-millionth truck and introduced an in-line six cylinder engine. Production of GMC trucks had continued through the twenties with engines supplied by companies including Buick who supplied GMC with their six cylinder engines.

Towards the end of the decade GMC offered a truck, the T-11, based on a Pontiac design that had only been offered for a single year and in this initial model even the Pontiac engine was used. A new model, the T-19, was introduced in 1928 and showed that GMC was also developing its truck designs. The T-19 was manufactured in large numbers, some 20,000 vehicles being made in 1928 and 1929. Later GMC started producing Buick engines specifically for its trucks with the bore and stroke altered to make them more suitable for use in commercial vehicles. These engines which were offered in different displacements would have production runs for more than twenty years.

Studebaker pickup truck production had not been resumed until 1927 when a new truck model was announced and subsequently produced until 1931 when the company again abandoned the production of trucks. In 1929 sales of International Harvester trucks had grown to approximately 50,000 and overall the public demand for pickup trucks was still growing.

The later years of the twenties also saw the development of a new phenomenon, that of the suburb. The growing availability of motor vehicles meant that people were now able to work in a city and commute in from its edges. This would gradually bring about a major shift in many aspects of life despite the oncoming depression.

Below: *By 1929 Ford trucks were available in colors other than black. One color on offer was L'Anse dark green, a shade specific to Ford.*

1925 Model TT Ford

This Model TT one-ton truck number 13,290,322 was built in 1925 and sold by the Vandemower-Taylor Motor Company of Denver to wheat farmer Clyde E. Jones of Nunn, Colorado whose name appeared on the title on March 11, 1926. It was supplied as a chassis cab and Jones had the six quarter lumer load bed built for carrying wheat. The truck has spent more than 70 years within 10 miles of Clyde Jones' farm and is now treasured by another farmer in Nunn, Dick Barnes.

Specifications

Owner: Dick Barnes
City: Nunn, Colorado
Make: Ford
Model: Model TT one-ton closed-cab truck
Year: 1925
Wheelbase: 124 inches

ENGINE
Model: In-line, four cylinder L-head
Capacity: 176.7 cubic inch
Ignition: Magneto

TRANSMISSION
Type: Manual

SUSPENSION
Front: Transverse, leaf spring, beam axle
Rear: Transverse, leaf spring, beam axle

BRAKES
Front: None
Rear: Twelve inch drums

WHEELS
Wooden spoked

TIRES
Front: 30x3 inch
Rear: 30x5 inch heavy service

PAINT & FINISH
Paint: 1925 Ford
Color: Black

Above: *From the left, Floyd Dahl, Leon Sandidge and Babe with the 1933 Ford V8 chassis cab that Floyd restored from the ground up with Leon's help. The load bed is made from teak and intended for hauling beet.*

Limp flags in the afternoon sun. Today's Bargain. '29 Ford pickup, runs good. What do you want for fifty bucks – a Zephyr?

THE GRAPES OF WRATH. JOHN STEINBECK (1939).

MASS PRODUCTION

FORD AND CHEVROLET slugged it out through the Great Depression even as overall industry production totals of automobiles dropped. Chevrolet introduced an in-line six cylinder engine and Chevrolet sales soared to the extent that they were outselling Fords. Ford retaliated with a V8 in 1932, the year total production approximated 1.3 million vehicles and America elected its first woman senator. Hattie Caraway, a Democrat, was elected to represent Arkansas. New for 1932 was the Model B Ford, subsequently to be nicknamed "The Deuce" which, despite being launched during the Depression, became one of the most famous of thirties' American cars. One of the main reasons for its popularity was that it came with an L-head V8 engine, although a flathead four was an option. The V8 endowed The Deuce with considerable performance which would subsequently make it a favorite among the hot rod fraternity. It has been said by hot rodders that The Deuce is one of the few vehicles that looks as good with its curved fenders fitted as with them stacked against the garage wall.

The V8 powered truck variant was the Model BB which also appeared in 1932. V8 engines were not new and were already in use in luxury cars such as the Lincolns, built by Ford but they were not available in mass produced cars and trucks.

The difficulty in manufacturing a mass-produced, and therefore cheap, V8 was in casting the crankcase block and cylinder banks as one unit. Up until 1932 the V8 was cast in three parts which had to be machined and fitted together. Against a background of the Depression the auto industry was suffering, even Ford had closed a number of his autoplants and laid off approximately 75,000 workers as his financial resources were over stretched. His pattern makers and foundrymen were working day and night to produce the complex V8 blocks, struggling to control 54 separate sand cores. The scrap rate was as high as 100% at times but eventually the casting problem was solved so that the affordable V8 became a reality. Of this breakthrough Henry Ford was able to say, "The V8 is the coming car for the majority of American drivers. As always, we have done the pioneer work. It will only be a short time until motor manufacturing practice will follow the trail we have blazed".

The design of the new Ford range progressed under Edsel Ford and designer Joe Galamb while engineer Gene Farkas redesigned the chassis in a way that eliminated the need for splash aprons between the body and running boards (one of the reasons it looks good without fenders.) When the 1932 Ford range went on sale, it consisted of ten car variants and four trucks. The latter vehicles were a sedan delivery, a Murray and Baker-Raulang bodied station wagon and two pickups. The pickups were a Murray bodied open cab and a closed cab truck. The sedan delivery (with a single side hung door rather than a pair, no back windows and no back seats as in a panel truck,) the Station Wagon Woody, and open cab pickup were

built in small numbers, production totalled only 2,371 for all three but 14,259 of the closed cab pickups rolled off the Detroit line. Most of these vehicles were four cylinder powered because the V8 was not available for them until late in the model year.

The Murray-bodied open cab pickup was assembled from parts of other Fords including Model A leftovers but the closed cab pickup featured a new allsteel body that shared styling and parts with the cars. Although sales of the 1932 models were slow, mainly

Below: *The wheels of the restored 1933 Ford were painted 1975 Toyota yellow, the closest match to the original. The wheels were fitted with vintage style Country Squire tires.*

as a result of the Depression and Ford lost $75 million, the new engine re-established Ford as the leading automaker.

The depths of the Depression were plumbed in 1933 as thousands of the dust bowl farmers of Oklahoma and the surrounding regions drove west in search of a better life. Ford's range for the 1933-34 sales season included sedan deliveries that followed the lines of the redesigned car range while the Roadster and closed cab pickup models remained

more like the 1932 range in appearance. Ford managed to stay ahead of Chevrolet in numbers of trucks sold despite Chevrolet's significant advances through the thirties. In 1930 for example, hydraulic shock absorbers, vacuum windshield wipers, electric fuel gauges and external rear view mirrors all became standard equipment in Chevrolet trucks. Chevrolet acquired a specialist truck body maker - Martin Parry Corporation - in the same year which led to the company offering a range of half-ton pickups, panel trucks

Below: Built for hard work, not drag strips, this '33 Ford chassis cab was equipped however with the optional V8, the V8 that endeared itself to hot rodders across the US.

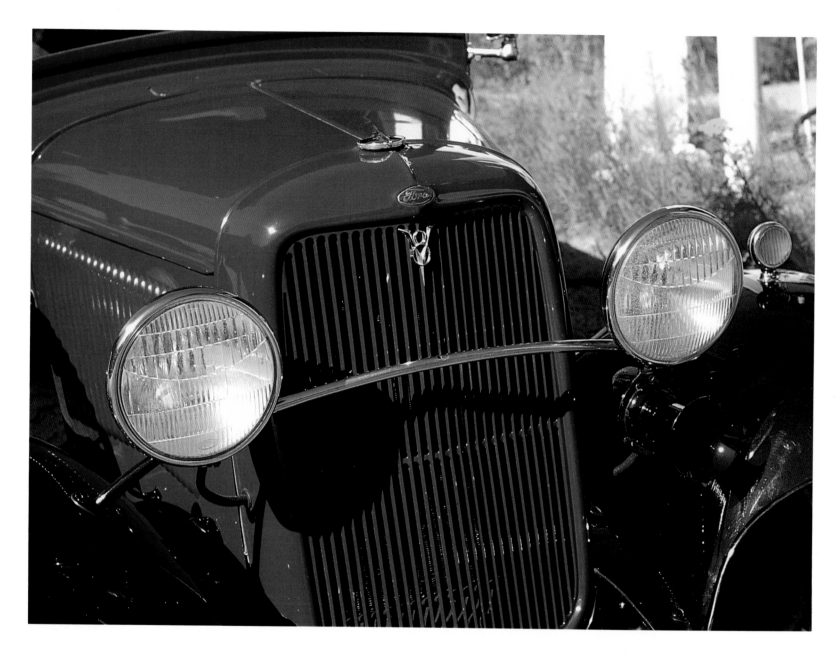

Above: *It is hard to imagine who could buy a new pickup in the early thirties as the Depression worsened. Despite this, Ford did announce the V8 in 1932.*

and canopy express trucks as factory models. The acquisition of Martin Parry would boost Chevrolet's sales in the light truck market far beyond the 32.7% sales share it had already achieved by this time. Through the thirties Chevrolet offered a range of colors, a synchromesh transmission and pushed its trucks hard through fleet sales. These improvements contributed to the company's market share climbing from that achieved in 1930 to 50% in 1933, the same year as it produced its millionth truck.

As the thirties moved on Chevrolet trucks became more streamlined and styled in the manner of its pas-senger cars, certain models shared the same front end sheetmetal. The range included larger capacity trucks including three-quarter and one-ton models. Progress continued and in 1934 Chevrolet trucks came equipped with hydraulic brakes – referred to in the slang of the time as "juice-binders" – and the cabs were built with one-piece steel roofs. This year saw the overall total number of trucks produced increase slightly over 1933. A range of trucks completely designed by Chrysler appeared in 1933. The new range included an in-line six cylinder engine, a feature that would endure until the sixties. The styling of the vans and fire trucks. In 1939, the pickup was to share its front end with Studebaker's redesigned car line.

IHC had expanded its truck line in 1936 to include seven basic truck models within its range. They all had styling similar to the 1935 models. This included a tall V-shaped grille, long hood with louvered sides, a tall cab and curved fenders that ran back to join the running boards. The smaller displacement trucks used Waukesha four cylinder engines while the larger models used an in-line six. A redesigned line of IHC trucks – the D-series – debuted in the spring of 1937. The appearance of the new models was considerably different as a result of redesigned grilles, two piece windshields and a fat-fendered appearance. The all-steel cab styling was referred to as 'turret-top styling' by its maker. This new range helped IHC increase its lead over Dodge and retain the third position in sales in the US with 30.22% of

Below: Julian Guzman from Greeley, Colorado owns this 1937 Ford Model 77 half-ton Series 830 pickup. The 77 designation identifies it as the 85 hp version.

the total truck market. The figure would drop considerably to only 10.24% for 1938 but surprisingly still leave IHC in third position. The IHC trucks continued almost unchanged for 1939 and IHC sales improved slightly to give the company 11.38% of the total US market.

Circumstances changed significantly again at Ford in 1938 when its trucks came assembled with a chassis that conformed to the specifications of the Society of Automotive Engineers' (SAE) recommendations which included both better brakes and larger diameter wheels. For 1938 Ford had also offered a range of one-ton trucks to complement its existing half-ton line. Matters continued to improve and by 1939 Ford trucks were equipped with "juice binders." The range had also been expanded to make it even more comprehensive with the addition of three-quarter-ton

models. These trucks featured a rounded radiator grille shell, even more rounded fenders and steel wheels instead of the laced wire items used until this time.

GMC was aware of the changing trends and its range was redesigned for 1939. The windshields of the vehicles became two-piece and although the grille remained vertical it was redesigned to incorporate heavier looking horizontal inserts. The company offered four six-cylinder powered, half-ton models on a 113.5 inch wheelbase and three similarly engined models with a 123.75 inch wheelbase. The half-ton models were designated the Series AC-100 and AC-102 trucks while the greater payload models were the AC-150, AC-250 and ACL-300. In the various capacities there were chassis, chassis cab, pickup and panel truck models and in the larger capacity trucks there

Right: *Charvon Walter in his 1938 Chevrolet Model HD three-quarter-ton truck near his home in Windsor, Colorado. The truck has been in his family for forty years.*

Left: *Ford was justifiably proud of its V8 engines and the V8 logo can be found no less than ten times on this truck. The emblem is shown here on top of the radiator grille.*

1933 Model B18 Ford

Despite the worst of the Depression, in 1933 in South Dakota someone purchased a new Ford chassis cab. The truck's original use is not recorded. The current owner, Floyd Dahl, has owned it for more than twenty years and Floyd carried out most of the restoration himself. Being a chassis cab model Floyd had to find and fit a rear body. A beet box from a similar vintage Chevy proved ideal, and it was the right size and exactly the sort of specialist rear body that would have been fitted to trucks like this.

Specifications

Owner: Floyd Dahl
City: Belle Fourche, South Dakota
Make: Ford
Model: Model B18 Chassis Cab Pickup
Year: 1933
Wheelbase: 106.5 inches

ENGINE
Model: L-head V8
Capacity: 221 cubic inch
Ignition: Coil and points

TRANSMISSION
Type: Three speed manual

SUSPENSION
Front: Transverse, leaf sprung beam axle
Rear: Leaf sprung, beam axle

BRAKES
Front: Drum
Rear: Drum

WHEELS
Laced

TIRES
Front: 6.00 x 16
Rear: 6.00 x 16
Country Squire

PAINT & FINISH
Paint: Owner
Color: 1970 Austin Healey red

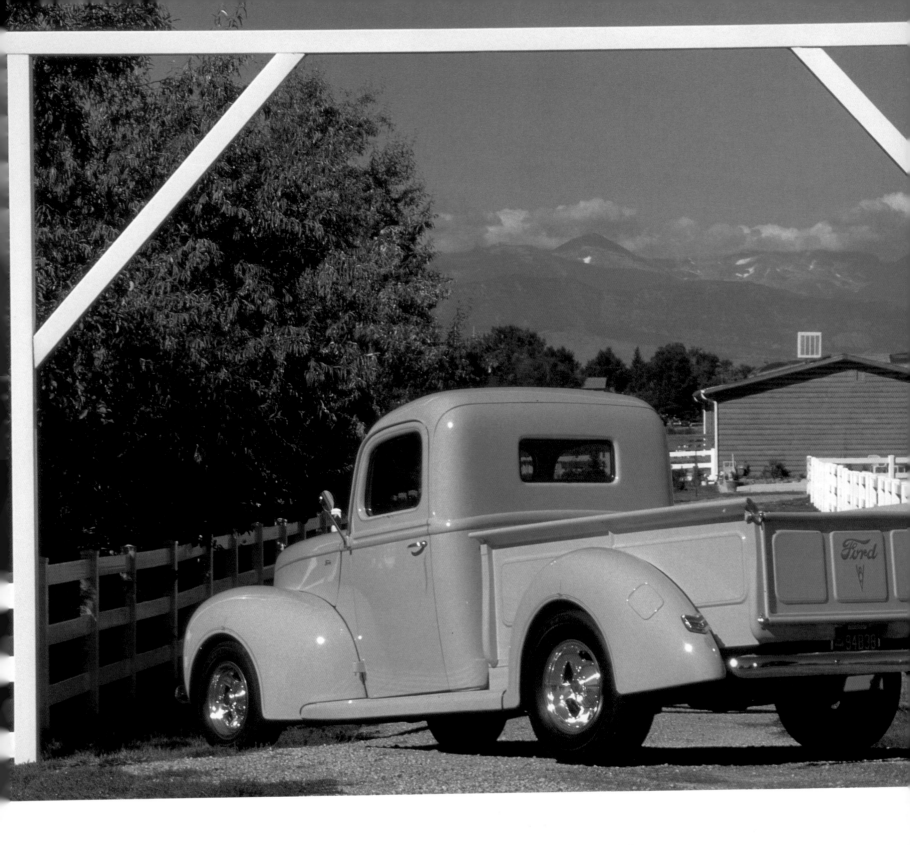

Above: *The 1940 Ford half-ton pickup is acknowledged to be one of the best looking trucks ever built. This example is Bob Crouch's street rod which has been subtly altered to incorporate the gas filler flap in the rear fender and fitted with Halibrand mag wheels.*

Commander Cunningham soon appeared in the civilian pickup truck that he used for a staff car. The pilot and co-pilot, Ensigns James J. Murphy and H. P. Ady, were wide-eyed with surprise as Cunningham drove them to his command post. It was obvious that they had not known how heavily Wake had been bombed.

WAKE ISLAND. DUANE SCHULTZ (1978).

A TIME OF WAR

FORD BECAME UNIONIZED on June 21 1940 but this continuing development in industrial relations was generally overshadowed by world events. The war raged in Europe and America was initially an uneasy bystander. In 1940 expenditure was allocated to enable the US Army to procure much needed motor transport. This was due in part to the fact that the earlier reorganization of the army intended that non-divisional cavalry in the form of cavalry recon squadrons would ride "point" ahead of the new divisions. Each squadron would consist of three recon troops and nine recon platoons that would be transported in a defined number of White and Dodge trucks, Scout and Command cars respectively as well as motorcycles. For the civilian market, new for 1940 was the "Forty Ford" range which is generally acknowledged as featuring some of Ford's most distinctive trucks ever. The new trucks featured styling similar to the Ford cars for that year with a graceful hood that extended forward to finish almost in a point. The rear sheetmetal varied, depending on the type of vehicle, in a range that included panel truck, pickup and stake bed trucks. There were half-, three quarter- and one-ton variants which had 112, 122 and 122 inch wheelbases respectively. The Marmon-

Herrington 4x4 conversion for Ford's three-quarter-ton Model 11D Pickup was an innovation. Willys Overland was producing similarly styled trucks with hoods that, like Ford's, finished in a point. The Willys trucks had progressed from a flat grille with the introduction of the Model 77 in 1937. This became the Model 38 in 1939 and the Model 441 in 1940. In the latter year the company produced a total of 32,930 cars, trucks and Jeeps.

IHC introduced its Model K truck during the fall of 1940 for the 1941 model year. The styling was modern and incorporated integral fenders that also housed the headlights and a small vertical grille and a rounded hood. The new series was powered by the "green diamond" in-line six cylinder engine. With only minor changes this design would take IHC up to the outbreak of war. A new line of Studebaker pickups was introduced for the 1941 model year and designated the M series. The series used a common cab and front end sheetmetal that was unique to the truck line. The truck was built with economic priorities in mind and the running boards were interchangeable from side to side to minimize production costs. The front and rear fenders were interchangeable on a given side for the same reason. An I-beam front suspension system was used on the 113 inch wheelbase truck that was powered by an in-line six cylinder engine. The company sold more than 8,000 M-series trucks in its first year of production.

The Japanese air strikes against Pearl Harbor on Hawaii, Guam and the Philippines on December 7 1941 pushed America into World War Two. The US entered the war by Act of Congress the day after the airstrikes. Within days the United States Marine Corps was fighting to hold Wake Island. The Marines' determined stand for sixteen days against overwhelming odds was the first sign, soon after the dis-aster at Pearl Harbor, that although the road to victory would be long and costly, America would ultimately win.

In the final years before American involvement in World War Two the GMC trucks were redesigned again and most of them were redesignated as CC Series trucks. The redesign moved the headlights out onto the fenders, saw a new horizontal barred grille fitted and incorporated the sidelights into the tops of the headlight cowls. The styling remained unchanged on 1942 models until production was suspended for the duration of the war. The outbreak of World War

Left: *The 1940s Fords featured a pointed hood and grille which incorporated a V8 hood ornament. Truck styling was almost identical to that of Ford's car line.*

Two saw White move to Scout Car production and Dodge produce a range of military vehicles. The latter's vehicles included a three-quarter-ton 4x4 chassis which served as the basis for weapons carriers, ambulances and command cars. This vehicle was to be such a success that a postwar version of it known as the Power Wagon was introduced for the civilian market.

The other truck makers also assisted in the war effort. During the conflict IHC manufactured a range of machinery, including half-track vehicles, for the Allied armies. The company produced more than 13,000 International M-5 half tracks at its Springfield

plant and also made a number of "Essential Use" pickups for civilians who required transport in order to assist the war effort. Willys Overland received a truck manufacturing stop order from the War Production Board on March 4 1942 and completely turned its attention to the quarter-ton 4x4 Jeep MB. Ford's civilian trucks were redesigned again for 1942 but then the company turned its efforts to winning World War Two. One of Ford's major contributions to the Allied cause was to turn some of its production capability over to building Willys MB Jeeps because Willys did not have the vast production capacity required. The

Below: *This street rod interior includes a late-model tilt column and a modern dashboard. Owner Bob Crouch built the street rod in Longmont, Colorado.*

Right: *The styling of the Ford truck was innovative at the time of its introduction. Notable in 1940 were the headlights in the fenders and their egg-shaped chrome trims.*

Far Right: *The rear fenders have been fitted with 1940 Ford passenger car tailgates. The truck is powered by a V8 and painted in Ford Regatta Blue.*

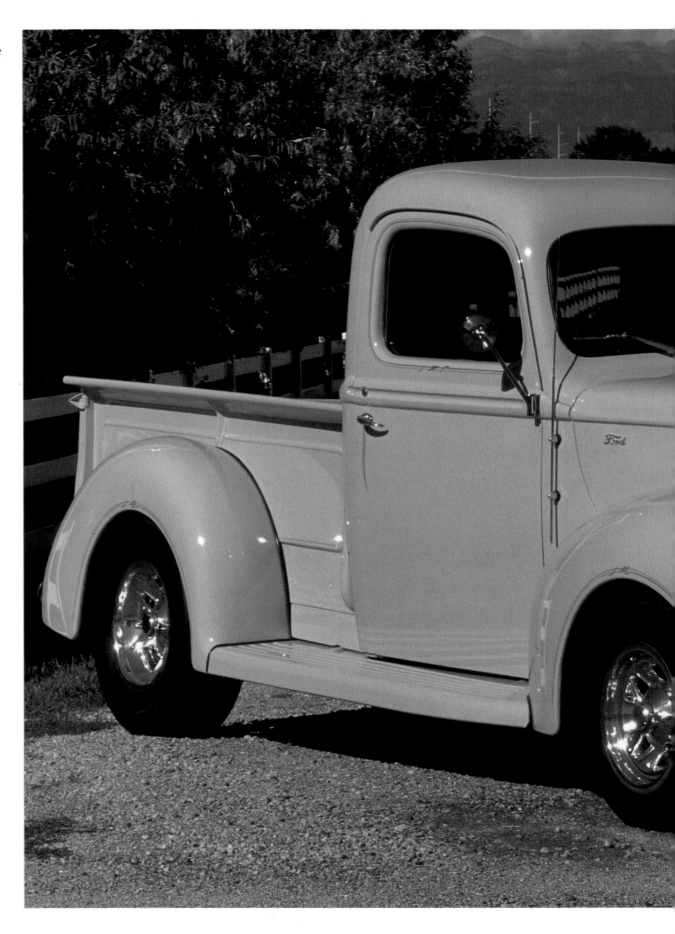

Ford-assembled Jeeps were designated Ford GPW and the company also produced an amphibious variant of the same vehicle which was designated the GPA. When the war ended Willys had built 358,489 MB Jeeps and Ford had built 277,896 of its equivalent, the GPW. The Ford Model GC was a military specification 4x4 pickup truck.

At Chevrolet, civilian truck production ended in January 1942 although the company later obtained permission to build a number of trucks. These were built to 1942 specifications and intended for high priority civilian use, until civilian trucks could start rolling off the Chevrolet lines again. It was 1944 before this could happen in large numbers. The numerous trucks produced for the Allied cause during World War Two meant that Chevrolet was the main supplier of 1.5 ton 4x4 trucks to the US Army for the duration of the conflict. The trucks were of a standardized design powered by a six cylinder in-line gas engine, driving through a four speed transmission and two speed transfer case. The chassis was of a steel ladder type with leaf sprung suspension, a steel closed cab of a conventional design and a cargo rear body with a canvas tilt completed this, the NJ-G-7107. All Chevrolet plants participated in the war effort with the exception of Saginaw which exclusively made spares for the civilian Chevrolets already on the road. Chevrolet of Canada also produced numerous trucks for the Allies including the C30 and the 1311X3. In addition to other vehicles, GMC produced a vast number of the famous 6x6 "deuce and a half" 2.5 ton trucks for the Allied armies. These trucks were available in soft and hard cab models with a cab not dis-

similar in design to that of the CC Series half-ton trucks. Studebaker assembled approximately 200,000 2.5 ton US6 6x4 and 6x6 trucks. Approximately half of these went to the USSR as Lend Lease equipment. The GAZ plant in Gorky, Russia produced a close copy of this truck in the postwar years. Studebaker also produced Wright Cyclone Flying Fortress engines and in excess of 15,000 Weasels. This was a light, fully-tracked military vehicle that was designed by Studebaker's engineers. Studebaker was another of the manufacturers permitted to produce a number of trucks for essential civilian use toward the end of the war. Chrysler made Sherman tanks while Pontiac made anti-aircraft guns.

Above: *Many Dodge Weapons Carriers were built during World War Two. This is a 1944 WC51, of the 2nd Armored Division 81st Reconnaissance Battalion.*

Right: *The three-quarter-ton Dodge WC-series vehicles were powered by an in-line six cylinder side valve engine.*

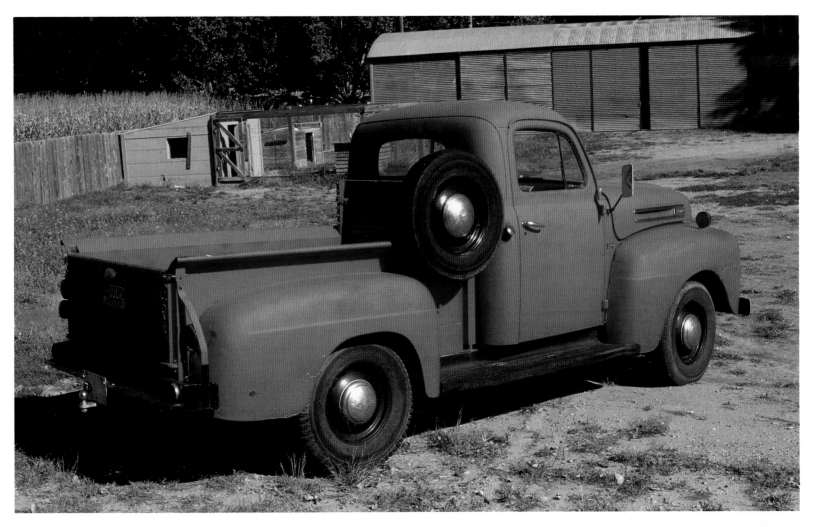

government for the war production and after the war Studebaker bought it from the government and prepared it for truck production. The initial postwar sales boom did not last long and before the end of the decade the number of trucks moving off dealers' showroom floors had decreased. To combat this sales decline, Studebaker instituted a year model registration procedure that meant a 1949 built truck could be registered as a 1950. This system was similar to that already employed by IHC. The result was that the smaller manufacturers were no longer forced to compete with new lines from the bigger manufacturers each fall.

The mud on the battlefields and supply routes of World War Two had proven the extraordinary ability of four wheel drive vehicles beyond all doubt. In light truck terms Dodge and Willys had proven four wheel

Above: *The Ford F-1 was one model in a range of trucks offered by Ford. The longer F-2 rated as a three-quarter-ton model. This is a 1951 model.*

Right: *The types of load bed offered on F-1 and F-2 trucks varied. While this is a stake bed type, there were also chassis cabs, panel trucks and platform models.*

drive technology and saw the way to further increase the versatility of civilian trucks. Willys was among the first to see the advantages that four wheel drive would offer commercial vehicle users and so offered a range of four wheel drive pickups alongside its Jeeps. The styling of the trucks differed from that of the first civilian Jeeps but the design of their grille and front fenders left no doubt as to which company had produced them. The pickup trucks featured a steel closed cab with a variety of rear body types being available including a stepside, a stakebed and a chassis cab to allow the instalation of specialist equipment on the back. The pickup range was complemented by a line of panel trucks and an estate car line. The four wheel drive models were capable of having power take offs fitted to the gearbox to drive machinery. The first 4x4 truck made by Willys rolled off the Toledo, Ohio production line in February 1948 and trucks continued to do so until 1963 with only minor changes over the years. The grille was later redesigned and a one piece windshield substituted for the two piece item originally used. It wouldn't be until the fifties that the major US manufacturers would include 4x4 pickups in their regular lines.

'Optimo City is the blur of filling stations and motels; the brief congestion of mud-spattered pickup trucks that slows you down before you hit the open road once more'

J. B. JACKSON. THE ALMOST PERFECT TOWN (1952).

THE FABULOUS FIFTIES

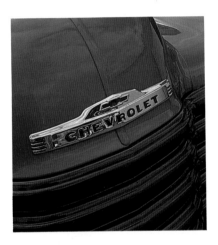

IN JANUARY 1950 a completely new range of trucks - the L-Series - was unveiled by IHC. The trucks were both restyled and re-engineered and the styling now incorporated wide, flat fenders, a less rounded hood and significant changes to both the radiator grille and trim. Under the hood was a new in-line six cylinder overhead valve engine. This style ran until 1953 when it would be superseded by the R-series which was a development of the L-series. The front end was again redesigned and become concave with an oval aperture. A two-tone paintjob was an option as was a model with a greater payload. The standard half-ton pickup was known as the R-100 and had a 115 inch wheelbase while the R-102 was the heavier truck with the same wheelbase. The R-110 was the longer wheelbase variant also available as the R-111 and R-112. These trucks were to remain in production until 1955 when the S-series would make its debut. The 1949 2R truck was a good seller for Studebaker so few changes were made for 1950, 1951, 1952 or the final year of 2R production in 1953. At GMC it was a similar story for 1951, 1952, and 1953 as only minor changes were made leading up to the major redesign for 1955.

The Korean War had started on June 25 1950 when North Korean soldiers invaded South Korea by crossing the 38th Parallel, the line at which the country had been arbitrarily partitioned in 1945. In response to the outbreak of this war the US Department of Defense reactivated the Ordnance Tank Automotive Center in Detroit, Michigan to again mobilize the automotive industry for war production. On January 15 1951 Dodge began building trucks for a military contract for example. Dodge built a truck designated the M37 for the new military contracts. It was clearly a development of the WC series of World War Two and similarly styled but upgraded. Most of the automakers had received military contracts of one sort or another but in excess of 8 million cars, trucks, and buses were produced in the US in 1950, estimated to be more than 75% of all the vehicles made in the world that year.

The Korean War continued into 1951 as the People's Republic of China sent troops and assistance to the communist North Koreans. In order to avoid raising the stakes too high, President Truman was forced to sack General MacArthur, the UN Commander in Chief when he talked of invading China. This escalation led to restrictions on the amount of certain metals including zinc, chromium, tin, and nickel that could be used by the American auto industry for work other than that related to defense. Chrysler and Cadillac were making tanks and GMC truck plants were assembling the M-135 6x6 truck for the US Army. Numerous other restrictions came into force as a result of this latest conflict, the National Production Agency (NPA) limited both car and truck production in order to ensure a continuous flow of equipment for the war. The NPA assigned a quota of trucks to each manufacturer based on its percentage market share. Dodge's NPA quota, for example, was 13% of the industry total. The Korean War dragged on through 1952, the year that Republican Dwight D. Eisenhower was elected president, and ended only after the agreement at Panmunjon in July 1953. The cost had been high, including 51,000 American dead and the face of world politics had changed. The Korean War had been the first confrontation of the big powers in the nuclear

Right: *Alison Thomas owns this 1952 Dodge B-3-B pickup which is painted to look as if it belongs to a fifties' hot rod shop in Santa Maria, California, hence the whitewall tires.*

Below: *The dash of the 1952 Dodge had unusual cowls for the speedometer and radio speaker. The truck was powered by an in-line six of 217.8 cu in displacement.*

age and was the model for the brinkmanship of numerous Cold War era conflicts to come.

The F-series trucks had carried Ford into the Fifties on a very firm footing and Ford became the nation's number two automaker, partially as a result of a serious labor dispute at Chrysler. The F-series underwent a redesign in 1951 when a redesigned grille was fitted. In 1952 two new overhead valve engines were made available, an in-line six and a V8.

The major facelift however was saved for 1953 and Ford's Golden anniversary, with its most major redesign in two decades. Most significant from the truck buyer's point of view was that the F-series was given the three-digit designations that have been used ever since. The F-1 became the F-100, the F-2 and F-3 became the F-250, and the F-4, slightly downgraded, became the F-350. This seems straightforward but there were, with the numerous options, a total of 194

Below: In 1955 Chevrolet introduced a stylized half-ton pickup as a limited edition. It was the Model 3124 Cameo Carrier and featured fiberglass slabsided rear fender sides.

Above: *The dashboard of the 1958 Transtar Deluxe. Studebaker offered many items as extra cost options on its range including ashtrays, extra sun visors and rear view mirrors.*

Left: *Steve Doerschlag rebuilt this custom 1958 Studebaker Transtar Deluxe with a hood and grille from a 1955 model. It has American Racing Equipment custom wheels.*

box was an option. The designations of 3100, 3600 and 3800 from the forties continued although some years earlier the 3700 had been added for the Dubl-Duty models.

The Chevy trucks that would become legendary however, were introduced as the second series redesign for 1955, albeit using the 3100 series designations. The new trucks featured wrap-around windshields, redesigned fenders and truck beds and had the option of a V8 engine. The 3100 was the half-ton commercial vehicle while the 3200 was a half-ton on a longer wheelbase, the 3600 was the three-quarter-ton and the 3800 the one-ton. The Dubl-Duty models used 3400, 3500, 3700 for its various versions. A Cameo pickup model appeared as a limited edition and the new design would endure with minor upgrades until the restyled model of 1958 was unveiled with its dual headlights.

Chevrolet had introduced the new models with what it described as "taskforce" styling that included new features such as the panoramic windshield that wrapped around the corners of the cab, the flatter hood, wing and roof line, as well as the egg-crate

Left: *As part of a minor redesign for 1955, Studebaker trucks powered by a V8 engine were fitted with a new hood ornament bearing the number 8.*

Right: *Colorado resident Steve Doerschlag also owns this two tone 1955 Studebaker truck which he has converted to a dualie (a truck with twin rear wheels) for use in connection with his work.*

grille. The trucks were only slightly upgraded for 1956 and would subsequently be upgraded again for 1957 in a similarly minor way.

The new GMC trucks were also considerably more angular than their predecessors. The front end featured a two bar grille reminiscent of passenger cars of the era and was complemented by hooded headlights and a massive chrome bumper. The GMC logo was mounted on the lower portion of the hood front in a stylized form. The cab was redesigned to incorporate a wraparound windshield and the higher front fender line ran right through the cab and doors. The new designs were designated as Series 100, 102, 150, 251, 252, 253 models reflecting wheelbases and payloads. The trucks fitted with the optional V8 were given an additional '8' suffix. In this way the half-ton model on a 114 inch wheelbase was a Model 100 while the V8 variant was the 100-8. The Series 150-8 trucks were three-quarter-ton trucks on a 123.25 inch wheelbase and V8 powered. Of these models, registrations for the 1955 calendar year totalled 84,877 vehicles.

The 1956 GMC models continued almost

unchanged from the 1955 ones although the V8 models were no longer listed as a separate series, the V8 simply became an option. The engines were increased in displacement to 269.5 and 316.6 cubic inches for the six- and eight-cylinder units respectively. A redesigned grille was the only obvious styling change for 1957 but for 1958 the range was redesigned in several small ways and a pickup body made by Wide-

Below: *The owner of this Studebaker Transtar deluxe has increased the truck's performance by fitting a 1957 Golden Hawk sedan McCullough supercharger.*

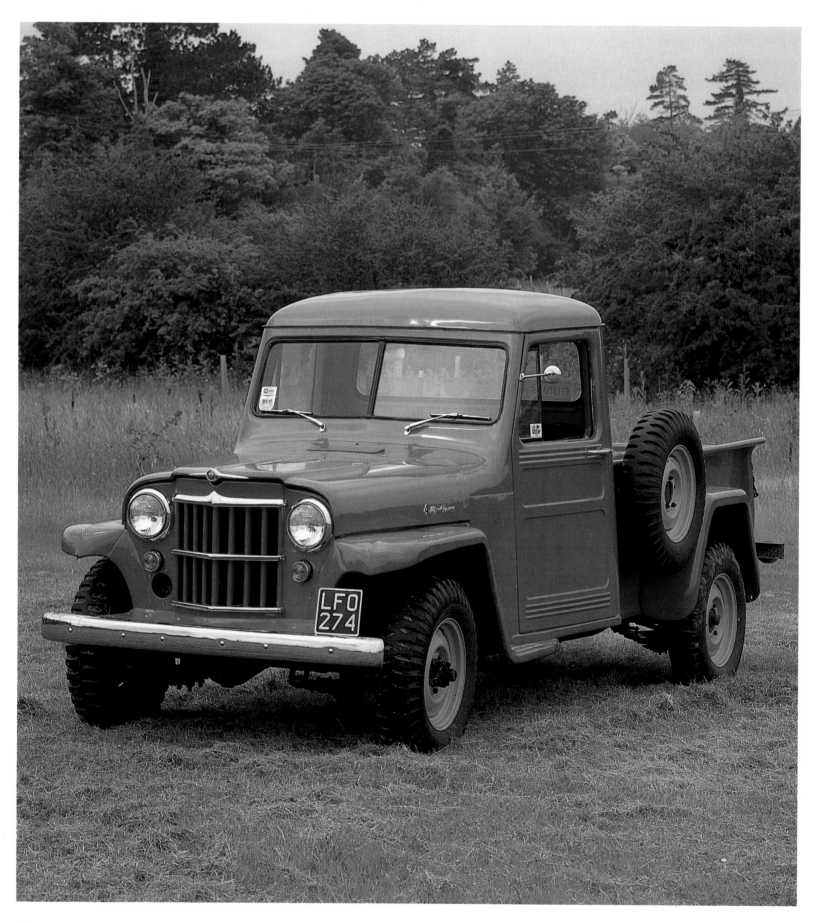

Left: *Barry Redman restored this 1957 one-ton four cylinder engined F4-134 4x4 pickup. It is of a design introduced by Willys Overland in the immediate postwar years.*

Far right: *The designers at Willys Overland combined the familiar flat-paneled appearance of the Jeep with the curves that were popular in the fifties as on this door handle.*

Right: *The interior of the truck is austere. It was equipped with a bench seat, a steering wheel with a Willys Overland logo in the horn push and extra gear levers.*

try various manufacturers produced futuristic vehicles. GMC's truck and coach division rolled out the Turbo-Titan, an experimental truck designed and built to use a gas turbine engine for power. Ford produced the similarly experimental Glidaire which traveled on a cushion of air rather than wheels. The company took the idea a step further and followed the Glidaire with the Levacar which like the Curtiss-Wright Aircar was also an air-cushion vehicle. By 1959 Chevrolet, as part of GMC, produced the Turbo Titan II, a second gas turbine powered truck and Chrysler experimented with an electro-chemical source of power while Cadillac experimented with radar for cars. Also hinting at future developments was the fact that 1957 was the year that saw the first imported VW trucks and vans take to America's highways.

Left: *Concave styling features were a feature of early sixties trucks and were incorporated into the front edge of the hood which also included the turn signals.*

pickups. The Champ and the Transtar went on sale in 1960 the Champ in both 4x2 and 4x4 models. Studebaker trucks were manufactured only until 1963.

The sixties were important years for Dodge who built a comprehensive line of pickups. The redesigned Dodge cabs were lower and wider than those which had gone before and mounted on new chassis with different wheelbases. Future revisions were minimal and included a switch from single to dual headlights and back again. In the range were Sweptline pickups, Sweptline Power Wagons and crew-cab Power Wagons. The company also offered a number of derivatives including a fully enclosed Power Wagon, known as the Town Wagon, in 1962.

The early years of the sixties were troubled ones for the American nation. On December 22 1961 James Davis from Tennessee became the first American serviceman killed in Vietnam and less than a month later on January 12 Operation Ranch Hand took place to defoliate parts of Vietnam using the chemical Agent Orange. The Bay of Pigs fiasco and the Cuban Missile

Crisis followed as Cold War tensions heightened. In August 1963 Martin Luther King made his historic speech at the Lincoln Memorial in Washington DC and in November President Kennedy was assassinated in Dallas, Texas. Lyndon Baines Johnson the Vice-President who was with Kennedy on the trip to Texas was sworn in as the 35th US president in Dallas.

Ford had entered the sixties with another redesign for the popular F-series trucks in 1961 which included a reproportioned body. By now it had single headlights, a horizontally barred grille and a wraparound windshield. This design lasted several years into the sixties through a number of minor upgrades such as the facelift for 1962 and new grilles for 1964 and 1965. The wheelbase was lengthened while the front overhang was shortened. In 1964 the Ford name was pressed into the tailgate. Long bed variants of the F-100 and the F-150 appeared in the same year aimed at those who wanted to carry camper shells.

International Harvester had made headlines with the 1961 introduction of the Scout, one of the first

Right: *The styling of the dashboard, instruments, and steering wheel of this 1962 Chevrolet was modern and making greater use of plastic materials and technology.*

"sport utilities," although that particular term had not been coined then. It was a boxy, small pickup with rounded corners and a truck cab designed to seat three. The tailgate hinged downward and the cab roof was removable. The grille was rectangular and single circular headlights were positioned at either side. The Scout was available in both two- and four wheel drive versions, rated as a quarter-ton and known as the Model 80. It was powered by an in-line four cylinder engine and constructed around a 100 inch wheelbase. The Scout proved to be a success and in excess of 28,000 were sold in 1961. The IHC C-series pickups was a comprehensive range and upgraded versions of the earlier B-series models. The C-100/C-102 models were half-ton trucks based on a 119 inch wheelbase,

C-110/C-112 trucks were three-quarter-ton trucks on a variety of wheelbases, C-120/C-122 were one-tonners also based on various wheelbases as were the C-130/C-132 models. Both the Model 80- Scout and the C-series of pickups were continued for 1962 with only minimal changes. Roll up windows were an option on the Scout and the doors were removable for off-road use and the windshield folded flat. There were similar models of the Scout for 1963 and 1964 although the pickup line was restyled.

The recreational user pickup market was growing rapidly during the mid-sixties and brought changes to the ranges offered by the likes of Chevrolet who, in 1965, introduced a 325 cubic inch V8 powered long box model suitable for demountable camper fitment.

Above: *Ford continued using its "Custom Cab" designation for luxury truck models into the sixties, including its 1963 F-100 models.*

Above: *Jason Grasseschi from Loveland, Colorado owns this flame red restored 1963 Ford. It has been fitted with custom, chrome steel wheels and radial tires.*

The company also introduced a camper special which had beefed up power train and chassis components. IHC was also aware of this growing recreational market for utility vehicles; a 1965 survey of IHC Scout buyers showed that around 75% of Scouts were purchased for non-business use and 82% of them were purchased in 4x4 form.

Looking further toward the future, in 1965 Chevrolet built another futuristic concept truck, the Turbo Titan III, with a gas turbine engine for power. It was displayed at auto shows and two years later Dodge displayed its concept truck, the Deora. The Dodge Deora was fitted with an internal combustion engine but offered car-like comfort in a pickup. In many ways these vehicles anticipated the sport-utility

market by at least fifteen years. Despite Chevrolet's use of a gas turbine engine in its concept machine its internal combustion engines had plenty of miles left in them and in 1965 registrations of its trucks exceeded the 500,000 level. It was a boom time for America's number one truck maker and a year later the company sold its 10 millionth pickup. Its trucks were redesigned for 1967 and optional interior packages including the CS and CST models were offered. Chevrolet felt that this redesign was, "the most significant cab and sheetmetal styling change" in its history and certainly the trucks acquired a much more modern appearance. They appeared longer and lower and much closer to the styling of cars of the time. This was as a result of the trend towards pickups for personal transportation and leisure vehicles as well as working vehicles. The trucks were redesigned to slant inward above the waistline and to incorporate a swage line that defined the wheel wells and body sides. The area of glass in the windshield and side windows was increased and the elongated appearance was reflected in the grille that featured two long narrow rectangular panels. The new C-10 was offered on two wheelbases in both Fleetside and Stepside forms and as either a 4x2 truck or a 4x4. The only noticeable change for 1968 was the addition of additional chrome trim and badges to the trucks.

Hot on the heels of this redesign came Chevrolet's first full size 4x4, the Blazer in 1969. The suspension arrangement on the Blazer was to use tapered single leaf springs at the front and multiple leaf springs at the rear. The 4x4 Blazer base model was powered by an in-line six cylinder engine although V8s were optional as were manual or automatic transmissions, power steering, power brakes and a removable fiberglass hardtop. The colors, exterior trim, interior trim and general equipment were not dissimilar to that used on the K-10 4x4 models of pickup.

The IHC Scout was partially redesigned and upgraded for 1965, a new grille, new hood emblems and a permanently fixed windshield were among these upgrades. The windshield wipers, pedals and numerous interior details were also improved. The Scout was still available in both 4x2 and 4x4 form although 82% of the Scouts sold in 1965 were 4x4 models. The company also found that half of Scout buyers had never bought an International before and that trade-ins against Scouts included a large proportion of both sports cars and station wagons. These findings influenced IHC who marketed Scouts with increasingly luxurious interiors and for 1966 offered in-line six cylinder engines and, later in the same year, V8 options.

In 1966 the Ford Bronco appeared in three styles, roadster pickup, sport utility pickup and wagon intended to compete for sales with both the Jeep and International Harvester's Scout. The Bronco was the

Left: *Ford, like Chevrolet, was offering more luxurious interiors in its trucks in the early sixties and assemblies such as the instruments were much more stylized.*

Right: *Vents were introduced to the front of the 1963 Ford below the hood and above the grille. The hood ornament is heavily influenced by industrial design.*

first light utility 4x4 built by Ford since its wartime production of the GPW Jeep. While the Ford Bronco was grabbing the headlines, changes were made to the company's truck range that included front disc brakes and optional air conditioning. Also new for 1966 was the change of base vehicle for the Ranchero, instead of using the Falcon platform it was now based on the Fairlane. The F-100 truck was restyled for 1967

but continued to be available as styleside, flareside, chassis cab and platform and stake models as well as two longer wheelbase models. The F-250 remained as the three-quarter-ton variant available with as many body types and two crew-cabs, namely a styleside and a chassis cab. The one-ton F-350 was offered as a flare-side pickup and a chassis cab but also in two wheel-bases with platform and stake bed bodies. There were also long wheelbase F-350 crew cabs in styleside and chassis cab variants.

Production of the Ford Bronco, International Scout and jeep models both reflected the trend toward recreational vehicle use and encouraged it, enabling owners to travel more on backwoods trails. The enthusiasm for such trips saw the arrival of specialist magazines, such as *Fourwheeler*. The development of these trucks later diverged into 4x4 and sport utilities.

The GMC trucks for 1967 were completely redesigned in both styling and engineering features. A number of safety features including seatbelts, four way flashing hazard lights and a dual braking system were included as standard. The overall shape was more slab sided and sharp edges had been eliminated in favor of rounded ones, giving a modern look to the trucks, something that was complemented by the simple radiator grille and dual headlights. Following this major redesign the changes for 1968 and 1969 were minimal although larger displacement V8s were available. By 1967 in excess of 800,000 American businesses depended on automobile use and more than 13 million people were employed in businesses that utilized buses and trucks. In the same year more than $13 billion worth of auto parts were produced for the auto industry by other industries and, reflecting the growth in recreational use of light trucks, more than 625,000 mobile homes and campers were produced. The number of mobile homes, travel trailers and truck campers produced the following year exceeded an estimated 818,000.

The war still raged in Vietnam and in 1967 the US Army was consuming 850,000 tons of supplies and 80 million gallons of gasoline monthly. At the end of January 1968 the Viet Cong launched the Tet Offensive against Saigon, Hue and other South Vietnamese cities and places such as Khe Sanh and Da Nang became committed to the pages of history books. In 1969 the US spent $28.8 billion fighting the Vietnam War and Chevrolet introduced the Blazer, a full size 4x4 ahead of a similar vehicle from Ford. The

Ford Bronco and Ranchero models continued through 1968, 1969 and into the seventies in similar configurations although subsequently the body styles of the Ranchero were redesigned several times, always in keeping with passenger car like styling. Four wheel drive transmissions were available as an extra cost option. In 1968 for example the 4x4 system added an extra $645 to the cost of both the F-100 and F-250 models. In that year the production of the entire range which had been introduced in the fall of 1967 was a fraction less than 415,000 vehicles.

For 1967 the IHC Scout was marketed with three

Below: *During the sixties the Power Wagon stayed in Dodge's range of four wheel drive form. This period brochure illustrates the payload models offered and their type of use.*

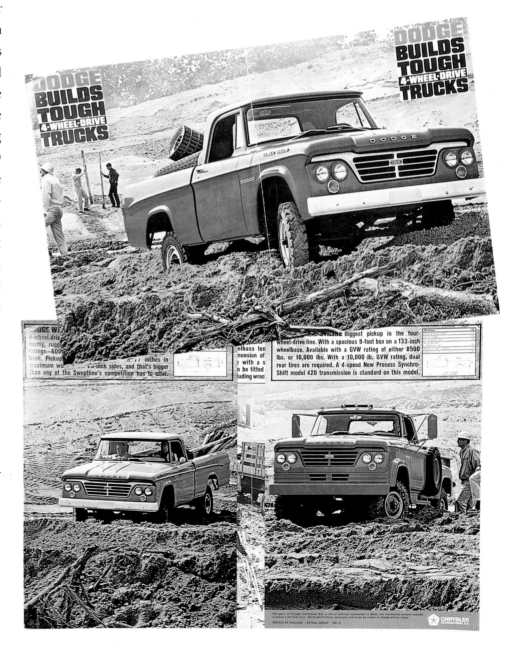

different interior and exterior trim levels, Utility, Custom and Sportop. The utility models featured bench seats and painted bumpers. The custom models featured a number of interior comforts including bucket seats, armrests, sun visors, vinyl trim as well as chrome bumpers and hub caps. The Sportop featured a slanted back roof hence its name, and inside had bucket seats and other luxury trims as well as chrome moldings, trim, and bumpers. Alongside these sport utilities production of pickup trucks and crew cab trucks continued in both two- and four wheel drive form. Little was changed for 1968 but the company

offered limited edition Scout models for 1969-70. The Scout Aristocrat included such features as two-tone paint and chrome custom wheels. IHC's line of conventional pickup trucks was redesigned for 1969 and the trucks were given a wide flat hood and slab-sided fenders, a design reminiscent of the still successful Scout models.

The last year of the sixties was the year that saw men, Neil Armstrong and Buzz Aldrin, on the moon as the US won the space race. It had started in 1961 when the USSR made Cosmonaut Yuri Gagarin the first man in space. Overshadowing this was something else that the US was embroiled in but seemingly could not win, the Vietnam War. In May 1969 units of the US Army and South Vietnamese forces attempted to take Hill 937 - Hamburger Hill - in the A Shua Valley east of the Laotian border. It turned into one of the bloodiest battles of the Vietnam War and provoked heavy criticism in the US as the hill had little strategic value. The Vietnam War became noted, among other things, as the first helicopter war in history and it is not stretching credibility too far to suggest that the Bell HU-1 "Huey" synonymous with images of the war was the pickup truck of the unfriendly skies. Combat troops, casualties and cases of supplies, the Huey trucked them all and more.

Above: *Mike Remley restored this 1964 Chevrolet truck from the springs up. It is finished in Chevrolet's Light Green which replaced Glenwood Green in that year.*

Right: *Mel Villegas' 1965 Ford truck is equipped with twin I-beam suspension and a V8 engine as the hood ornament (left) indicates. It has also been fitted with a camper shell, a longstanding and popular truck accessory.*

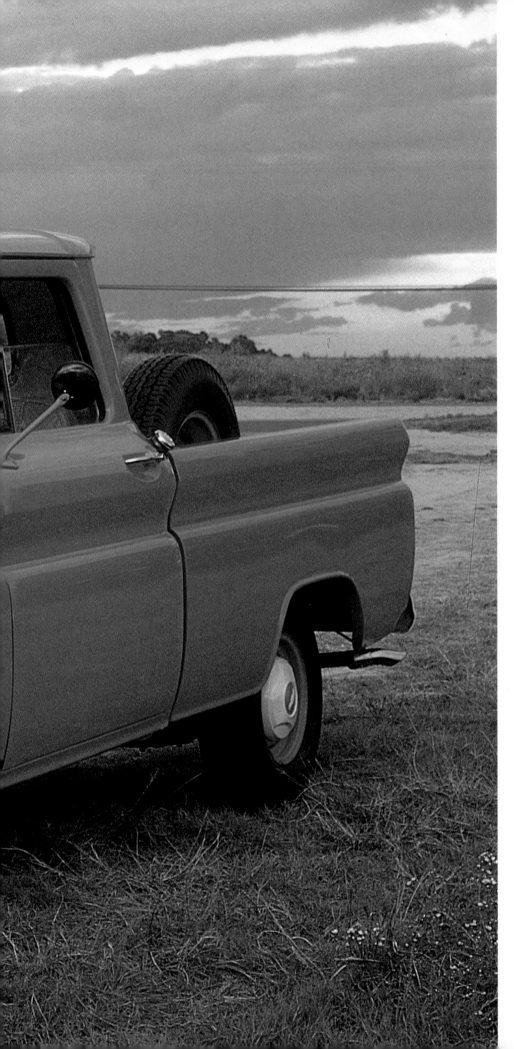

1964 Chevrolet C10 Fleetside

This truck was completely restored from the frame up by its owner Mike Remley from Greeley, Colorado. In 1964, the year it was manufactured, this variant of the C10 series was one of 193 models in that year's Chevrolet truck range which was based on numerous wheelbases. The windshield pillars had been redesigned to slope in the opposite direction of the 1963 models but other modifications were minor. They included a redesigned grille, hubcaps, and instruments.

Specifications

Owner: Mike Remley
City: Greeley, Colorado
Make: Chevrolet
Model: C-10 Fleetside Pickup
Year: 1964
Wheelbase: 115 inches

ENGINE
Model: OHV V8
Capacity: 283 cubic inch
Ignition: Coil and points

TRANSMISSION
Type: Three speed manual

SUSPENSION
Front: Leaf sprung beam axle
Rear: Leaf sprung beam axle

BRAKES
Front: Drum
Rear: Drum

WHEELS
Kelsey Hayes 15 inch steel

TIRES
Front: 6.70 x 15 inch
Rear: 6.70 x 15 inch

PAINT & FINISH
Paint: Chevrolet
Color: Light Green

Above: *Leon Sandidge from South Dakota with his Chevy truck. Toward the end of the sixties truck styling became less curved and continued like this into the seventies.*

'He turned now to face her, exhaling a filmy cloud of cigarette smoke. 'And what happens when the money runs out?'
'Okay, then let's spend it here,' Mally said. 'Let's use it to buy a pickup truck, an old car, something unobtrusive. We can take the back roads, turn ourselves in at a precinct.'

THE GAUNTLET. MICHAEL BUTLER AND DENNIS SHRYACK (1977).

MAGNUM FORCE

THERE HAVE BEEN suggestions that the design of American automobiles reflects how good the country is feeling about itself on an almost year-by-year basis. It may be an apocryphal indicator of the nation's outlook but when viewed in the most general terms it does appear to have some credibility. Truck and car styling was flamboyant in the euphoric postwar years but decidedly lackluster in the uncertain years of the early seventies. The seventies would see President Richard M. Nixon scaling down and subsequently ending US involvement in the Vietnam War faced with ever increasing opposition to the war. At the time the US automakers were also operating numerous assembly plants around the world including 50 in South America, 60 in Europe, 17 in Africa, 40 in Asia and 27 in Oceania. Although these figures would have shifted significantly by 1973 there was concern about the volume of US domestic auto production when compared to the number of imported vehicles. In 1970 imported vehicles numbered more than 2,000,000 while domestic factories produced in the region of 8,200,000 vehicles. This latter figure accounted for 15.9% of America's steel production as well as 41.2% of the iron and 8.2% of the aluminum.

Chevrolet's Blazer was the first of the full-size, big-engined vehicles based on the idea of a shortened 4x4 pickup chassis. The Blazer first appeared during the 1969 model year in both six- and eight-cylinder engine types and was designed to be assembled from existing and proven Chevrolet and GMC light truck components that would ensure it quickly gained market place acceptance. In 1970 Chevrolet's sales were adversely affected by a UAW strike against GMC that lasted 58 days and reduced the American Gross National Product (GNP) by $9 billion. The highest specification Chevy Blazer until 1973 was the CST - Custom Sport Truck - and the Cheyenne Specification package was introduced in 1973 while a roll bar became standard in 1975. All the 4x4 models were leaf sprung front and rear. Two wheel drive Blazers were produced from 1970 onward but proved less popular than the 4x4 models. GMC put a new product - the GMC Jimmy - on the market in 1970 in order to reap some benefit from the growing recreational vehicle market. Much of its styling was taken from the GMC pickup truck range and it was virtually identical to the Chevrolet Blazer except for some trim parts. The Jimmy was available in both two and four wheel drive configurations with a removable hardtop over the

Right: Chevrolet offered two ranges of trucks in the early seventies; the full size line as well as compact import badges such as Chevy LUV vehicles.

rear load bed and front seats. It was designated C1550 and K1550, the prefix varied according to the type of transmission, C indicated 4x2 models while K was 4x4. For the first years of the seventies the conventional GMC trucks continued to receive only minor upgrades for each year but they, along with the Jimmy, were restyled for 1973.

The introduction of the IHC Scout II came in 1971 and production started alongside that of the Scout and the company's conventional light truck range. The new Scout, introduced in the spring, had been redesigned and now incorporated power brakes, power steering, air conditioning, automatic transmission and a V8 engine. The body was longer and lower than that of the previous model and sales exceeded 30,000 in the first year of production. For 1972 the Scout was discontinued while the Scout II continued, upgraded only in minor details such as changes to the radiator grille. The front end of the Scout II was redesigned again for 1973 as was that fitted to the IHC range of trucks. At this time IHC was America's

fifth largest truck maker behind Chevrolet, Ford, Dodge and GMC in that order.

Right from its 1966 introduction the Ford Bronco was a trend setter in the four wheel drive and sport utility sector of the truck market and the first truly mass-marketed 4x4 in the US. It featured an innovative coil spring suspension system and an in-line six cylinder engine with a V8 available as an option. The Bronco was otherwise basic and options such as power steering and automatic transmissions were not available until 1973. The Bronco lasted in almost its original form until 1977 when it was replaced by the upsized Bronco based on the Ford F-150 pickup chassis and was closer in concept to the Chevy Blazer.

Apollo 15 put wheels on the moon in 1971 when the astronauts James Irwin and David Scott drove the Boeing-constructed Lunar Roving Vehicle (LRV) several miles on the moon's surface during their mission. Closer to home the trend towards the recreational use of trucks was growing ever stronger. In 1972 the popularity of mobile homes, camper trailers,

Below: *The stylized badge on the fender of a Chevy LUV – LUV is an acronym for Light Utility Vehicle.*

truck campers, travel trailers and truck covers was such that a rise in pickup sales was recorded as part of the surge in the sale of recreational vehicles (RV). Pickups were used to haul trailers and carry camper bodies. At the time it was noted that the average RV family spent 10% of its time using the vehicle and that the family unit was made up of four persons headed by a white collar worker. This was in marked contrast to the pickup truck's distinctly blue collar heritage and, of course, its continuing use in both industry and agriculture.

In 1972 the method of construction used for the car-styled Ford Ranchero was changed. To make it

bigger and stronger it now featured a separate chassis and body as opposed to the previous car-like mono-coque construction with an integral chassis. A sports version was known as the Ranchero GT Sedan-Pickup and the Squire variant featured imitation wood panels along the sides and a number of other trim detail upgrades. The base models were powered by an in-line six while the base GT models featured a V8. There were numerous V8 options too that included 302, 351, 400, 429 cubic inch displacement engines as well as both manual and automatic transmissions. That year's styling changes to the conventional F-100 and F-250 truck models were considerably more lim-

Below: *This K-10 is described as a Scottsdale which is a specific trim level. Brushed aluminum was a common feature in the interiors of late seventies trucks.*

upgraded and fitted with disc brakes on the front axle. Exterior styling remained unchanged on Ford's range of pickups and minimal upgrades elsewhere. The range continued with only a minor facelift for 1976, America's bicentennial year. The long-running Bronco was designated the U-150 in 1978 and redesigned to standardize more parts with those of the F-series trucks and to change its appearance. Sales more than doubled in the following year and took Ford into the eighties along with the further redesigned fleet of F-prefixed trucks. In 1976 a survey in *Popular Mechanics* magazine found that 53.9% of

Ford van buyers used their vehicles for recreation.

In 1977 Chevrolet saw its sales exceed one million per year. After 60 years of truck manufacture the company had made a total of 21,850,083 trucks. The LUV models had put Chevrolet firmly into the mini-truck market and were to maintain the company's strong position in this sector until the introduction of the compact Chevrolet S-10 in 1981. The 1977 Chevy LUV was available in two wheelbase lengths, 102.4 and 117.9 inches and was, according to the sales brochure for that year, "tough enough to be a Chevy." The LUV was powered by a four cylinder

80 bhp engine and according to the Environmental Protection Agency (EPA) estimates returned 34 mpg on the highway and 24 mpg in urban use. Numerous options were available including the Mighty Mike decal package, a rear step bumper, an automatic transmission, air conditioning and an AM/FM radio. Interior trim levels included the more luxurious Mikado package with a further option of high back bucket seats in place of the bench seat.

The K30 4x4 one-ton models were added to the full size Chevrolet line up in 1977 and with them came Bonus Cab and Crew Cab models. The grille was redesigned and power windows were added to the list of available options. The K prefix continued to indicate a Chevrolet 4x4 model and by 1977 it was possible to buy a GMC K3500 Crew Cab Wideside 4x4 pickup, the 4x4 option would have added $1248 to the base price. Other variations were available, such as the Desert Fox trim option of 1978 which reflected the popularity of off-road desert racing in the US.

Indy Hauler trucks were also built to mark the GMC company's involvement with the Indy 500 when GMC trucks were the official speedway trucks during the famous race. In 1978 the Chevrolet truck chassis was slightly redesigned to make space to allow the fitment of catalytic converters, initially required only in California. There were a number of minor styling upgrades for 1979 that including changes to the grille. In 1977 the front end of the Ford Ranchero was redesigned to incorporate stacked rectangular headlights while production of the other Ford trucks continued in a similar style to before. The variety of options, variations and body types meant that it was possible to buy vehicles such as a F-150 Ranger XLT Flareside 4x4 Pickup. XLT was a trim level and Flareside was Ford's description of its stepside models. The Plymouth Trail Duster vehicles received a minor facelift for 1977 when the grille was redesigned to incorporate horizontal bars and vertical signal lights while the Plymouth badge was shifted from the

Below Left: *Bonanza was another trim-specification used by Chevrolet for its full-size trucks in the seventies. This is the fenderside badge.*

center of the grille to the face of the hood. The standard engine was an in-line six cylinder. IHC's Scout II remained in production however with few changes beyond a slightly different range of optional V8 engines. The production run of the Scout II would last until 1980 after which the company concentrated solely on the heavy truck market. The last years of Scouts saw the models increasingly aimed at the sport utility market although there were pickups made including the Scout II Terra Compact Sport Pickup.

For 1978, the year Americans bought an estimated 4 million pickups, the Ford Bronco was completely restyled and now closely resembled the full-size Ford pickups which had also been restyled for this model year. A rectangular grille was set higher, the amber lights were set below the headlights, and a new bumper was installed. The types of cab and transmission in 4x2 or 4x4 configurations were retained as were the F-100, F-150, F-250 and F-350 model designations. Matters continued in a similar way for 1979

Below: *Zak Wilson of Wheatland, Wyoming driving his modified Chevrolet which he has used in the truck class at local tractor pulling competitions.*

Below: The truck features a custom nudge bar, bug screen and four KC Daylighters in pink covers mounted on the rollbar. The Chevrolet emblem is known as the "bow tie."

although the trucks were fitted with rectangular headlights. The Plymouth models were left unchanged for 1978 after the 1977 redesign but options were offered, such as different seats, tinted glass, tilt steering column and a CB radio integrated with the AM/FM stereo. New for 1979 was the Plymouth Arrow, a down-sized mini pickup made by Mitsubishi in Japan for Plymouth. The Arrow was powered by an in-line four cylinder engine of 122 cubic inch displacement.

A sport package for the same truck was also offered that included bucket seats, extra dashboard gauges, spoked sport wheels and decals.

Dodge introduced a factory custom truck in 1978 known as the Li'l Red Truck which followed from its black-painted Warlock model of 1976. Much of the seventies is remembered as the "musclecar" era and although it was almost over by 1978 the Li'l Red Truck was a fitting swansong as the first muscletruck. It was

Above: *Zak Wilson's truck is powered by a 454 cu in displacement OHV V8 engine, the largest one manufactured by Chevrolet and renowned for its performance.*

based on the D150 truck powered by a 360 cubic inch V8. The prototype had W2 cylinder heads and a Holley four barrel carburetor and would run mid-14s out on the quarter mile strip where the musclecars decided who was boss. Eventually a slightly lower performance version - it would run mid-fifteens - was offered to the public through Dodge dealers. It was finished in red, trimmed with the "adventurer" package, wooden bed details and gold decals. The truck was offered for two consecutive years, in 1978 2,188 were made and in 1979 5,118. The second year models had dual square headlights at each side of the grille while the earlier had single round lights. The later model featured a catalytic converter as the emission regulations tightened. Three Li'l Red Trucks ran in the infamous Baja 1000 desert race during 1979 in conjunction with Walker Evans, Dodge's noted off-

road racer. Two made it to the finish in La Paz, Mexico while the third suffered a punctured radiator and was forced to retire.

The 1980 range of Chevrolet trucks introduced in the fall of 1979 was as large as ever and included two and four wheel drive Fleetside and Stepside models as well as two and four wheel drive Fleetside Sport and Stepside Sport models, two and four wheel drive crew cab and bonus cab models, two and four wheel drive chassis cab models for specialist rear bodies such as wrecker trucks as well as the C-10 diesel pickup and the heavy duty BIG-10 pickup. "Name the job there's a truck here to match" said Chevrolet. Four trim packages were listed, Standard Custom Deluxe, Scottsdale, Cheyenne and Silverado. The latter was the most luxurious. The eighties were just around the corner and times were changing.

1979 Chevrolet K10

This half-ton Chevrolet was originally modified in South Dakota and is typical of a style of 4x4 truck built for off-road use. It features a six inch suspension lift and three inch body lift which allow the fitment of massive wheels and tires, as well as improving the approach, departure and ramp-breakover angles of the truck. The lift required new Rough Country shock absorbers and the tires required changes to the ring and pinion gears in the differentials, and a Trailmaster steering damper assembly.

Specifications

Owner: Jeff Murphy
City: London, England
Make: Chevrolet
Model: K-10 Stepside CK10703
Year: 1979
Wheelbase: 117.5 inches

ENGINE
Model: OHV V8
Capacity: 350 cubic inch
Ignition: Coil and points

TRANSMISSION
Type: Three speed auto. Two speed transfer box. Part time 4x4

SUSPENSION
Front: Leaf sprung beam axle

Rear: Leaf sprung beam axle

BRAKES
Front: Disc
Rear: Drum

WHEELS
Mickey Thompson Alloy

TIRES
Front: 44.18.5.15 Gumbo Monster Mudders
Rear: 44.18.5.15 Gumbo Monster Mudders

PAINT & FINISH
Paint: Custom
Color: Various colored panels

Above: *As Chevrolet moved into truck production for the eighties it retained the basic boxy shape of its seventies models but redesigned components such as the radiator grille. The option of diesel power was a sign of the times.*

Down at the Ford place in Clanton he was known as the last man in recent history to pay cash for a new pickup truck. Sixteen thousand cash, for a custom-built, four-wheel drive, canary yellow, luxury Ford pickup.

JOHN GRISHAM. A TIME TO KILL (1989).

THE NEW MILLENNIUM

WITH THE BENEFIT OF hindsight it seems that the eighties started in a low key way. The presidential race between Ronald Reagan and Jimmy Carter was ongoing. The Philadelphia Phillies won their first World Series baseball tournament in 98 years. The arrival of a new Chairman – Lee Iacocca – at Chrysler made the news in the automotive industry in the early eighties. As the decade opened Ford advertised its F-100 as the "first new truck of the eighties" and produced redesigned models including a number of "custom" paint options with contrasting panels. The model designations remained unchanged so it was, for example, possible to buy a Ford half-ton F-150 Custom Flareside 4x4 pickup. The Ford 4x4 models featured a new front suspension system known as the Twin-Traction Beam independent suspension. In the same year the Ranchero pickup was dropped from the Ford range. Sales of early eighties models generally dropped because of the poor state of the economy. Ford continued to sell its compact, Mazda-built Courier pickups and the company turned some of its attention to more fuel-efficient vehicles. Styling of the F-series trucks remained unaltered although there were minor upgrades including removing the word "Ford" from the front edge of the

hood and installing the famous oval blue logo in the center of the grille.

In March of 1982 the downsized Ranger pickup made its debut. With styling similar to the F-100, it had become a model in its own right rather than a trim option for an Effie and just a year later the Bronco II made its debut and more than doubled sales.

The 1979 Chevrolet range of full size trucks had been the C- and K-series pickups, crew cab pickups, fleetside sport pickups and Big Dooleys, the latter being a large capacity truck with dual rear wheels. This range continued into 1980 with only minimal changes. A range of trucks included the basic van, a Sportvan, a Nomad van and a Caravan and in addition there were the Suburban and Blazer models in two and four wheel drive variants. This range was complemented by the compact Chevy LUV and the El Camino models. In the eighties the company was to adopt a new strategy and stop manufacturing heavy duty trucks, preferring instead to concentrate on the medium and light duty markets. The Silverado models were given rectangular headlights but the major changes came in 1981. GMC made only cosmetic changes to its range of trucks as the company entered the eighties although the square patterned ice-cube tray radiator grille remained. A styling extra-cost option that showed the direction in which auto-styling was headed was the dual stacked rectangular headlights either side of the grille in place of the single circular ones fitted as standard. The half-ton models retained an in-line six cylinder engine as standard while the other base models included a V8 engine as standard.

This program of minor upgrades continued into the 1981 models, for example, detail upgrades were made to the transmission of the 4x4 variants and the front sheetmetal of both Jimmys and pickups was redesigned to make it more aerodynamic and therefore improve fuel efficiency. New for 1982 from GMC were the S15 model trucks on which work had begun in 1978 as a response to the increasing popularity of the smaller sized imported trucks such as the Chevy LUV which was really an Isuzu with Chevrolet badges. The S15 was similar in size to the LUV and by 1983 there were 4x4 and extended cab models available. The downsized GMC Jimmy was based around the S15 and featured a tailgate and two doors on a 100.5 inch wheelbase and was a four wheel drive vehicle. The Chevrolet S-10 of 1982 was a compact that replaced the Chevy LUV and was available in two and later four wheel drive.

Above: *Crewcab models such as this Chevrolet C20 three-quarter-ton found favor with many commercial users, including the USAF, the original owner of this one.*

Right: *As well as manufacturing the Commanche trucks, Jeep experimented with Jeep-based trucks including the CJ8 Scrambler models and later this CJ10 truck.*

Dodge shifted production to more aerodynamic pickups and a down-sized model, the front wheel drive Rampage, a sport truck.

New for 1984 from Ford was the down-sized Bronco II sport utility designed along similar lines to the compact Ranger pickup. The F-100 was discontinued with the F-150 becoming the base model in a range that still included the F-250 and F-350 pickups and by the middle of the decade The Ranger and Bronco II were established in Ford's range of light duty trucks along with the full size F-150, F-250 and F-350 models.

For 1984 the limited edition GMC Indy Hauler pickup, to commemorate the Indy 500 motor race, was based on an extended cab S15 model. It was one of numerous options offered that year. The full size

GMC truck models continued into the mid-eighties with the same general appearance as had gone before although the program of sequential upgrades continued. Refinements were made in two areas, suspension and engine. Pickups in both wideside and fenderside variants continued to be manufactured and as a result of increasing awareness about gas-mileage, diesel options were introduced into the range.

The real news from Ford for 1986 was not about its range of pickups but the introduction of the Aerostar XL passenger van. Bronco IIs and Ranger pickups remained in the range as did the F-150, F-250 and F-350 models and after the disappointing sales of the early years of the decade Ford performed well. It had both a record sales year and regained the number one position in US auto sales. The Ford F-series ran

Above: *By the eighties, Ford's range of F-150 and F-250 models looked like this Styleside truck. The regular cab F-250 was offered with the eight foot Styleside box.*

Right: *By the beginning of the nineties, the Ford F-150 had become more streamlined and featured bumpers and headlight surrounds that were color-keyed to the truck.*

Left: *The 1993 high performance F-150 Lightning with a 351 cu in displacement V8 engine was introduced by Ford to compete with Chevrolet's sport truck, the SS. This Lightning belongs to Ray Kelly of Farmington, New Mexico.*

through the eighties, albeit with considerable changes, but remained as Ford's prime trucks intended to compete with Chevrolet during the first half of the nineties. The US economy as a whole was improving although in January 1987 it was noted that the farming economy was generally declining. It was accepted that the small independent farmer was disappearing and being driven from the land by falling prices. The number of farms was down 9% from 1975 making it the worst family farm depression in 50 years. Such a decline would, of course, affect the local economy in rural areas and decrease the number of pickups sold.

Over the course of the next decade the pickup truck market would shift considerably and sport trucks and sport utilities were to become mainstream America's major auto purchases. The compact Chevrolet S-10 was at the forefront of this trend. By 1991 the S-10 and C-series pickups and their respective Blazer and Suburban sport utility derivatives were as important as each other in the Chevrolet model line up. The nineties generation of the C- and K-series trucks were available with gas and diesel engines, short and long load boxes, regular and extended cabs and in three levels of trim, namely Cheyenne, Scottsdale and Silverado. There was a similar degree of choice for purchasers of the S-10 compact pickup with the exception of the diesel powered variant. The varying trim levels were referred to as Standard and Tahoe and there was an additional Baja off-road trim package for 4x4 models. The S-10 Blazer came in two or four door models with choice of 4x2 and 4x4 transmissions and featured an Electronic Fuel Injection (EFI) V6 engine. The trim levels offered were the same as those for the S-10. The full size Blazer was V8 gas or diesel powered with a choice of Scottsdale or Silverado trim and either two- or four wheel drive.

The APV - All Purpose Vehicle - was a new addition to the Chevrolet light truck range which included the Astro passenger truck, the Lumina APV and the Sportvan. A spectacular Sport Truck from Chevrolet completed the 1991 range although it was originally introduced in 1989 and was a truck that harked back to the musclecar era of the seventies. It was the 454 SS which was a 454 cubic inch V8 powered C1500 Fleetside pickup finished in Onyx Black.

By 1993 the 454 SS Chevrolet truck was faced with competition from Ford in the shape of the Ford F-150 Lightning which was powered by Ford's smaller displacement 351 cubic inch V8 albeit in a tuned form. Automotive magazine comparison tests of the time gave the Ford the lead in terms of all-around-use but the 454 SS Chevrolet was beyond doubt the leader in "muscle truck" terms. The Ford line up for the early nineties was comprehensive and based

around three models; the F-150, F-250 and F-350 with maximum gross vehicle weights of 6250 lbs, 8600 lbs and 11,000 lbs respectively. The three sizes of truck have correspondingly increasing payloads of 2145, 3915 and 5890 lbs. There was a choice of four body styles; Regular Cab, SuperCab, Crew Cab and Flareside and three trim levels: S, XL and XLT. That accounts for 36 different pickups before the engine options are considered. There were six different engines ranging from the standard 4.9 liter in-line six through a 5.0 liter V8, a 5.8 liter V8, a 7.3 liter indirect injection diesel V8, a 7.3 liter indirect injection turbo diesel V8 to a 7.5 liter V8. That took the number of F-

Below: *The F-150 Lightning was built around the F-150 Fleetside model and badged as the performance model. This one has aftermarket billet alloy wheels.*

Ford Model A Roadster

Old trucks make great street rods and Chuck Hill has owned this Ford for thirty years in which time he has driven it more than 122,000 miles. He's rebuilt it several times to keep up with the changing street rod fashions and this is its nineties incarnation. It is a combination of classic Ford parts and classic street rod items with nineties touches. The sheetmetal is old Ford. Classic street rod parts include the ARE five spoke wheels. The aluminum parts and aqua-colored paint are nineties.

Specifications

Owner: Chuck Hill
City: Longmont, Colorado
Make: Ford
Model: Model A Roadster Pickup
Year: 1929
Wheelbase: 103.5 inches

ENGINE
Model: 1967 Ford V8
Capacity: 289 cubic inch
Ignition: Coil and points

TRANSMISSION
Type: Automatic

SUSPENSION
Front: Transverse, leaf sprung tube
Rear: Mustang leaf sprung live axle

BRAKES
Front: Hydaulic disc
Rear: Mustang drum

WHEELS
American racing equipment alloy

TIRES
Front: 175/14 Radials
Rear: 255/70/15 Radials

PAINT & FINISH
Paint: Custom
Color: 1992 Ford Ranger Aqua

INDEX